TROPHY *Wife*

ERICA GRIER

This book is dedicated to the woman that's afraid of greatness. You don't need permission to be great. You were born with a Kingdom birthright. You will always be your greatest enemy. Get out of your own way and walk in what's rightfully yours! Go through the process and come out shining! Get happy about your life because it's about to get really good!

CONTENTS

Foreword

ERICA GRIER'S DEBUT BOOK, *Trophy Wife*, is an emotional journey through tests of unwavering faith and unconditional love. To know Erica personally is to know a woman who is a vessel of intuitive wisdom. Erica's supermodel looks are no competition for her beautiful heart – a heart that desires to help every woman who experiences life's most devastating betrayal. Infidelity is a humiliating secret that many wives experience but hide in shame. Erica understands that life's most challenging moments can be the biggest opportunities for growing closer to God and your husband.

In *Trophy Wife*, Erica courageously shares her life story with transparency and authenticity. Reading her truth on every page is like having a deep conversation with your best girlfriend. It is soul-filling, life-affirming, and wise way beyond her less-than-forty years. Supported by carefully selected verses from the Bible, Erica's counsel is a healing salve for hurting hearts and wounded marriages. She gives you hope for recovery and renewal. She reminds you why marriage is sacred and why the devil's purpose is to destroy it.

After reading *Trophy Wife*, you'll be prepared to fight for your marriage and win. With time, prayer, and unrelenting work as a couple to repair your bond, you'll be able to trust again. You and your marriage will become whole again. Life will be beautiful again. *Trophy Wife* is proof.

Angela G. Solomon

Introduction

"You're just a trophy wife."

I'LL NEVER FORGET THOSE WORDS spoken to me. At the time, they carried so much negative weight, but today, they are rejuvenating! Empowering, even. That day, I stared at my phone, trying to search for and gather the words to redeem myself. As I recall that moment in my mind, it left me feeling as if I had been cut in the deepest place of my soul.

Prior to introducing her to my world, I had become a well-respected and decorated businesswoman. My sole desire was to uplift and empower women, not put them down. Anyone who knew me also knew that I loved my husband and my children, and would do anything for them. I was one who worked very hard for them, almost literally to death. As a dedicated wife, I contributed financially so that my husband could focus and work full-time to create residual income for our children. As a full-time entrepreneur, those times came with very low lows that left my income as our primary source. However, those were days of my past at the time of the insult. I became a full-time stay at home mom and wife. I walked away from my career in order to be obedient to God's call to raise our children and focus on our family. Still though, flesh is flesh and my ego, perhaps even pride of

13

what used to be, made her comment feel demoralizing and demeaning... and ultimately those feelings magnified in her eyes, reducing me to a "just a trophy wife."

I thought to myself: *"She must not know who I am."* And so... I told her about myself: my most exceptional qualities and attributes. Hmph! I even told her that I and only I was the reason she was also on our business team! There! I told her! Until I realized I had fallen right into the trap. "What trap," you ask? The trap the enemy put in place to plant doubt and insecurity, and to grow the insatiable need to have to prove myself. This growth of doubt caused me to forget who I was, and even worse, I forgot who God said I was. *"How could I be so stupid?... I gave her what she wanted, and in turn, she's eating this up right now."*

"You're just a trophy wife."

Those words, spoken from the other woman. The woman with whom I blindly shared my husband. That is just it; she was **the other woman**, although I wasn't aware of this yet. Those words cut me so deep that day. That phrase, *"trophy wife"*, with all the negative stigma associated with it, became the biggest insult I ever received in my life! Although there are so many young women who strive to have a label like this one, I saw it very differently.

The other woman had a goal of hurting me and squelching me into a small, tiny insignificant box. A box of failure and worthlessness to justify her actions with my husband, and sadly, it worked. Temporarily though. God had been working on me for a couple of years prior to my husband's infidelity, changing my perspective of what a wife is and reshaping me to become what He intended wives to be all along. Even more importantly, He was preparing me to become HIS wife. This other woman knew, and the enemy knew how to hit me in my most vulnerable space. However, I was already on the journey of transforming from a *good wife* into a *godly wife*, without even knowing it. Up to this point, I had constant battles going on in my heart. Battles like, "Career vs. family?" or "Purpose vs. responsibility?" Seeing my husband work with women who sacrificed their own family for a career, while I stayed at home raising our children, in obedience to God, struck a sore spot in me, and it was a cord that was played often. The enemy knew exactly how to expose my fears and insecurities.

At the time of our conversation, I had no idea she was having an affair with my husband. However, the moment I ended the call, the Holy Spirit dropped these words in my spirit: *"She was right... in part."*

Trophy Wife, according to Webster's Dictionary, is an attractive young woman married to an older successful man. A wife by the world's standards is defined as a woman, a female partner in marriage. God says *"a man's greatest treasure is his wife. She is a gift from the Lord*

(Proverbs 18:22 CEV)." The Amplified Version (AMP) says: *"He who finds a true and faithful wife finds a good thing and obtains favor and approval from the Lord."* And God says in Proverbs 31:10 *"a wife is an excellent woman, one who is spiritual, capable, intelligent, and virtuous; who is he who can find her? Her value is more precious than jewels and her worth is more precious than rubies and pearls (AMP)."*

I AM a trophy wife! My husband's gift and treasure. The moment he called me his wife, was the very moment he received favor and approval of the Lord! Oh, but I am so much more.

Thinking about what God may consider a *"trophy wife"*, brings to mind The Oscars. Though many compete in specific categories, only one name is called to win. The winner did the necessary work and showed themselves approved and worthy of winning according to the standard set by the members of the Academy of Motion Pictures Arts and Sciences. Kind of like this: man is the actor, but God is the director AND the president of the academy. His reward of man's obedience to His lead in part is a wife, a help-meet, his good thing, his treasure! A major key to unlocking his purpose and destiny. And out of all her other contenders, she chose him. He won! So, in essence, the other woman was right. And to take it one step further, I realized that she too was someone's good thing. She had just forgotten that SHE was worth far more than rubies.

A ruby is one of the most precious gemstones because

it is very rare, even more than a diamond. Somewhere in her journey, she forgot her worth, and those insecurities she carried were transferred onto me. I fell for it. I took the bait. I was vulnerable and gave access for those venom-laced words to seep into my heart and my mind. Little did I know that God was going to use it for good and allow this scenario to serve as the foundation of my ministry, and this book.

And we know that all things work together for good to those who love God, to those who are called according to His purpose. Romans 8:28 NKJV

I have a hope that my story will help other women find their purpose and strength hidden within the layers of pain. It doesn't matter if the pain is inflicted by betrayal similar to mine, or if it is the consequence of the hardships of life, love, and/or relationships. As women, we have all been through something painful. It is in the essence of who we are, and it is a part of our DNA.

Silence keeps us in bondage. The key to someone's freedom from this pain, are the words they choose to speak. The power is in your mouth. It is in your story. And this is my story: the making and becoming of a trophy wife.

Part I:

THE *Molding*

ACCORDING TO MERRIAM-WEBSTER: Molding is an example to be followed; to mold is to give shape to (malleable substance); to determine or influence the quality or nature of.

When I also read Psalms 139:13-16 (NKJV), it tells me that before I was born God created a mold for me. That mold being my life and His design of it.

How wonderful is it to know that before we existed in the flesh, God created a one-of-a-kind mold specifically for each of us?

Our life was shaped before we took our first breath.

The afternoon I told my mother about Rahsaan's infidelity, she wept. Now I've seen my mother cry many times before. However, there was something different about this time. I wondered what was going through her mind and questioned if I made the right decision by telling her. I didn't want feelings to step in and cause judgment and scorn towards Rahsaan. Then she said, "Are you going to leave him?" My response was simply "I don't know." Every passing moment brought different thoughts than the previous. I changed my mind depending on how I felt at that given time. I was confused. It was her next statement that made me even more confused. She said, *"Don't leave him. He loves you, and he's a good husband and father. Try to give him a second chance. You don't want to have any 'what ifs.'"*

My childhood was simple...thinking simple in my most sarcastic voice ever. My parents were divorced, resulting in a single parent household. Although they were married for 18 years, they were separated for maybe 14 of them. I never knew why my mother left my dad. I never bothered to ask. The day I remember in my furthest memory was the day we left him. I remember starting kindergarten sometime shortly after and we were settled in with my great-grandparents. Like Rahsaan and I, they were childhood sweethearts. She loved my dad, and I know he loved her. They probably still love each other till this day. But theirs is a story of tragedy and disappointment. My dad had fathered a son while they were dating, and even though they eventually had me and married, the birth of my older brother may be something my mother never forgave him for.

What I do know is that the separation sent my father chasing after the wrong things. At one point he was in the Marines, and then he was not. He began a life on the corner. In Baltimore, that is selling drugs, also known as hustling. My father ultimately became a user of his product. He was in and out of jail most of my childhood, and well into my adult life. One thing for sure, I often wondered how different all of our lives would be if she had stayed with him. Confused, I asked her, *"Why did you leave?"* She said, *"Because your father changed, and I simply didn't want to be married anymore."*

There it was. My decision was simple. Rahsaan really did not change much during his ordeal in a way that made me question his love for me or his commitment to our children. He still showed me affection and we still made love. There were few moments that made me question what he was up to, and raised my eyebrows, but overall, I attributed them to stress of providing for our family. We had a newborn baby, so his one-offs made sense to me.

"Did I want to be married?" That was the million-dollar question; not whether if I loved him. Or whether I could forgive him. Or even if I could grow to trust him again. The burning question was whether I wanted to remain married to him. My answer was yes. I learned in our early years of marriage that love, trust, and forgiveness are things we give one another through the help of God. Not the help of our family or friends, but through God. I learned that the moment I rely on Erica, and all her habits and thinking, I struggled with moving forward. So, I had to rely on God's help as if my sanity depended on it because it did! And His help came through me saying "Lord, help me." It took practicing replacing a negative thought with a positive one and as I grew in my spiritual walk, replacing those negative thoughts with what God said from His word. We are transformed in Christ through His word to love, trust, and forgive. Those parts seemed easy to do because I submitted my will to God's will and even more easy when things were on the *"for better"* end of the scale, rather than the "for worse". It was staying

married that was confusing because I could follow my flesh and leave at my own will.

On that early morning, I had a much-needed conversation with God. I poured my heart out to Him. I poured my anger and confusion out to him as well. Rahsaan pleaded with me to stay; to give him a second chance. He said he would make me fall in love with him again. That was his primary strategy: to make me fall in love with him again and never lose it. Because, after all, loving and falling in love with someone is easy. It is staying there and building from that level that is difficult. He suggested counseling, sleeping on the floor, even quitting our business. I listened to and considered all that his ideas.

In my conversation with God, a piece of my childhood was revealed as a part to a puzzle, the bigger picture. It was brought to my recollection. This piece was the one that started the day we left my dad and moved in with my great-grandparents. This piece had a name, and it was Delphia Fowlkes, affectionately known as Mama-Stell, my great-grandmother. She was my very first authentic example of the 'Proverbs 31 Woman'. Her husband, my great-grandfather, trusted her greatly. She purchased fabric and made her own clothes. She taught me how to hand stitch garments, thread a sewing machine and sew. She taught to cook and preserve fruit, and even how to clean fish. She grew most of our food right in her backyard gardens. She was first to rise, making breakfast every day.

Every. Day. Day in and day out, she played old spiritual hymns and often fell asleep at the dining room table with her Bible open in front of her. We walked most places, for she believed as long as God continued to bless her legs to walk, she will use them. Her front door remained unlocked and her home was opened to any family, church member, or neighbor in need of food, shelter, a word from God, or all three. One of my fondest memories was watching her sit with neighbors, along with city officials and plan 'Block Parties'.

Although she taught me the Word of God, her biggest lessons for me were caught. Her walk as just as genuine and authentic as her talk. She practiced what she preached. I simply observed all that she did and was. I saw her do everything unto The Lord. She loved Him and was obedient to Him until the day she died.

That day, I spoke with God and wept, questioning whether I could remain married. He reminded me of the example He had woven and carved into my early childhood, through Mama-Stell. The example of what a Godly woman looks like and how she put her concerns in His hands. I vaguely remember my great-grand parents having any disputes or major problems. I was either too young for adult drama or they did a good job at covering it up. They were married for over 50 years until my great-grandfather's death. And THAT stands for something. From that reflection, longevity is what I wanted from their marriage for my own. My great-grandparents were of a different generation and mindset. And even though they stayed through thick and then and it seemed perfect to me, I had no idea what they went through in her early years, if they experienced anything at all. From that reflection, I wanted the same for my household. I wanted peace and no dysfunction in our household for our children as I had living with them.

God had shown me how my experiences growing up without my dad, seeing his brokenness shaped me. Even though I did not believe Rahsaan would abandon our kids, I also did not think he would ever humiliate me and break our vows. But he did. I couldn't leave anything for chance.

God sat with me and allowed my life to play out from childhood up unto that present dreadful day. He showed me all the instances, the times and experiences that prepared me for that very moment. All the good and bad and the hurt and joy were woven and carved into my mold.

I thought of all of the *'coincidences'* (although I know they weren't coincidences but rather divine appointments orchestrated by God) of my relationship with Rahsaan. We were both the only children to single mothers until the birth of our siblings at ages 13 and 15. We both lived with our grandparents at some point in our childhood, which allowed us to see marriage up close and personal. We loved music and had a fondness of live plays and musicals. He was the first person I confided in about my mother's drug addiction and my painful dislike of her new husband. He eventually faced that same road of substance abuse with his mother and I became a shoulder to lean on, just as he was for me.

God reminded me of how our dreams lined up and the vision he gave us as kids. Sadly, we both had a parent who was HIV Positive. The short version of Rahsaan's story begins with an absentee dad, then boy reunites with absent dad, then dad dies shortly thereafter from HIV. Seeing his pain allowed me to open up and share my own pain of my mother's testimony, of living with HIV and knowing that her story would end sooner than most. The day he buried his dad he held my hand the entire time. Some years later we heard Bishop TD Jakes say, "True love is knowing who you want to hold your hand when you are burying your parents." God reminded me of this series of events, a series of events that Rahsaan and I uniquely understood and how they all were carved into my mold.

The molding process that a trophy undergoes is one of the most important parts. Only the sculptor knows what goes inside of the walls of the mold, inside of the curves and tight spaces. In the process of making a trophy, gold is poured into the mold and set. The mold holds all of the details and secrets; the 'indentations' (good and bad experiences) and 'curves' (those times God spared us of tragedy, the close calls). Those good and bad experiences are what gives us wisdom. Our faith comes through the times God 'curved' us from something meant to harm us; the things seen and unseen.

The word trophy is derived from the Greek word *'tropaion'*, which comes from the verb trope, meaning to *'rout'*. In ancient Greece, trophies reflected war victory and were created on the battlefield at the place where the enemy had been defeated. That day, I started to see how God had been molding me as a 'trophy wife' all along, in preparation for this battle.

Catch that!!

I was molded and shaped, to reflect victory, being created on the battlefield at the place where the enemy had been defeated!!!

This battle, the attack of infidelity on my marriage and my very existence, had already been won. The 'trophy' had already been created with my mold in the very place the enemy was defeated. Do you get that, my sister? Your mold is already set. You can't see it but know that God fashioned it in resemblance of the place the enemy attacked, fought, and was defeated.

It's reassuring to know that.

Count all your parts as joy, every little detail of your mold! Look into the indentations and curves. That is where God hid HIS wisdom. Wisdom is needed to push through your present trials and attacks. God equipped you with everything you need. And if that isn't enough, remember in Romans 8:26-28, Paul says, *"Meanwhile, the moment we get tired in the waiting, God's spirit is right alongside helping us along. If we don't know how or what to pray, it doesn't matter. He does our praying in and for us, making prayer out of our wordless sighs, our aching groans. He knows us far better than we know ourselves, knows our pregnant condition, and keeps us present before God. That's why we can be so sure that every detail in our lives of love for God is worked into something good (MSG)."*

There were so many times I said I would never stay in a broken marriage. God said to me: "Check your mold and see all of the marvelous examples I set before you. Do you think I did not put everlasting power and endurance in your mold? Do you think I do not have a hand in your marriage? Try me. Use what I deposited in you when I formed you in your mother's womb. Let me show you what I will birth through you and your marriage."

I remembered being pregnant with Yasmine. We were so afraid. How were we supposed to take care of a baby and we're hardly not even taking care of ourselves? How? A baby is a huge responsibility, one we were not mentally, emotionally, and I later found out physically prepared for. We began contemplating an abortion and researched clinics and decided on Planned Parenthood, in downtown Baltimore.

I waited until the day before to tell my mother what we decided on. She very kindly said to me when I told her

I was pregnant, "I respect whatever you decide to do." Rahsaan picked me up around 8 am. We sat in silence the entire ride. I checked in and took my seat next to him to complete my registration. Tears soaked the papers as Rahsaan massaged my thigh, perhaps to steady my nerves or let me know he was there. I just remember staring at the first line: name and date. I couldn't think straight. I begged God for a sign. One that assured me that I was making the best decision. The waiting area was gloomy and had a chilling atmosphere. We just sat there. Both of us screaming on the inside, afraid to speak to each other out of fear of disappointing the other. There I sat, crying out to God, "please forgive me. Show me that I am making the best decision." Nothing. Then I thought "you have great plans for me. Surely this baby is of MY doing, but I know you work all things for the good of us who love you. Whatever your will is for this, I will know."

It felt like an eternity had passed before they called my name. "Erica...Erica...Erica, you don't have to do this." A familiar hand laid next to Rahsaan's on my thigh, and I looked up to see my mother in law's face. Her face soaked with tears and exhaustion and compassion in her eyes. She was out of breath. It took me a minute to focus on what was going on. There we were, the three of us sitting in a once full waiting room alone. Where did everyone go? It was as if time stood still. No one was at the desk either. Just the three of us. She sat down on my right and repeated: "you don't have to do this."

Then I broke and released all that had built up inside of me. I stood up and I felt relief. I felt God, saying "I got you. Do not fear. I am with you." We walked outside and with tears in his eyes, Rahsaan looked at me and said "a baby is here so that means God wants it here. I don't know how, but I know together we will be ok. I'm glad you didn't go through with it. I'm scared, but I know we will be ok."

Perfect, right? If I had any questions of his level of commitment, they all went out of the window. We had no idea what was ahead of us. The challenges we were walking into simply by saying "Yes" and giving God control of the situation Hurdle #2shortly arrived and proved temporarily that our flesh can get the best of us, but ultimately our spiritual strength conquers all. I learned that I wasn't physically prepared, but I was, however, spiritually ready for her. And here's how it all showed up: The obstetricians informed me around twelve weeks that she had very high chances of being born with Down's Syndrome. She had an abnormal amount of space between her eye sockets, and her first and second toe, as well as a flat facial profile. She also had what appeared to be a hole in the left ventricle of her heart. I was twenty years old, wondering how and why. They brought us before a team of genetic counselors, and we sat for an hour or so as we were educated on the realities of the livelihood of a person with Down's Syndrome. Twenty years old, being taught that she wouldn't learn beyond a two or three-year-old.

They told me that she would never obtain a career beyond a grocery store or a warehouse, restocking shelves. Now that I think about it all, I wonder why in the world would they say all of that and apply so much pressure on me.

> *"But Lord you said to trust you.*
> *But I don't know how to deal with this.*
> *We said yes, we didn't abort her and we're still*
> *going through something? This is scary."*

After much prayer, I agreed to an amniocentesis. That procedure is one of minimal pain and maximum concern. A needle, guided by ultrasound, is inserted through the mother's abdomen and a sample of cells from the placenta are retrieved. This test checks for missing or abnormal chromosomes. I was back in a cold room, this time about sixteen weeks pregnant while a technician inserted a large needle into my belly to withdraw amniotic fluid. Holding back tears, I heard The Lord say, "fear not for I am with you." That gave me comfort. I remembered that it was in that moment, I gave my unborn child over to The Lord. I thought whatever is in His will for her, I accept. We had to wait seven long days for her results.

In that one week, the enemy tried to test me over and over. But I decided to remind the devil that he couldn't have my thoughts. He couldn't have my peace. He couldn't have my strength, and I fought back. I fought back the best way I knew how: with my hands and the Word of God. I would place my hands on my belly and repeat 'no weapon formed against you will prosper. God has plans for you, plans to prosper you and not harm you, but give you hope and a future." I had peace because I knew that since God gave her to us, He already equipped us with what we needed to step into victory.

It is the same with my marriage. It was God's will that Rahsaan and I were together. He aligned our paths those many years ago. He knew before either of us existed that we would be one in covenant with Him. There is no question that our marriage is ordained. God spoke it. You should believe that your marriage is also ordained. That God wrote your names together in Heaven and aligned your paths on earth, to unite and carry out a kingdom assignment.

Yasmine's report came back free and clear, as I knew it would. She still had the hole in her heart, but I was not worried about that at all. The enemy was worried about it though. He threw another attack. Or maybe God was just strengthening my faith and preparing/molding me for the fights ahead. Shortly after our victory over Down's Syndrome we were shown an abnormality within my placenta. I had a complete placenta previa. A complete placenta previa is when the placenta blocks the baby's way out during delivery. It was improperly positioned. And considering I was six and a half months into my pregnancy and already three centimeters dilated, on top of standing on my feet working, I was considered a high-risk patient for preterm labor and placed on restricted bedrest. The complete placenta previa threatened of the possibility of maternal and fetal death due to severe hemorrhage if I went into labor. I was in a war, for my body and for my child. I would anoint my hands and rub my stomach, this time while singing praises unto The Lord. Twenty years old. Yep, that young.

Here is where God stepped in and showed out: at my 37-week visit the technician dropped the doppler and said, *"oh my God."* She left the room and reentered with more doctors. They had smiles on their faces and one even had tears in her eyes. They congratulated me and told me I would be able to deliver vaginally, and all of my restrictions were lifted. My placenta was in its right position and the hole that was in her heart completely closed!! One doctor said *"this is a miracle. Last week you were at 100% covered. We were certain of c-section delivery. Today it is as if the complications never existed."*

Three weeks later I delivered a healthy baby girl. She had two eyes, ten fingers and ten toes, and she cried out loud. Today she is in the top 10% of her graduating class, serves on the teen ministry at our church, is studying to be a lawyer, and participates on both the debate team and mock trial. She sings, is in theater, and loves writing poetry, with hopes of releasing a book of poems in the future. Yasmine is a world changer. She is the manifestation of love, God's love, the same love that healed her and birthed her.

You must look for the glitter in the hard situations you have gone through. The glitter is the gold dust that settled from what you were refined in. It is those victories that may have been downsized due to growth and progress. And the glitter is the remnant of what you thought would take you out. Look for those shiny reminders and memories that reveals your victories. Sometimes the glitter is gold.

Although two entirely different situations, both my pregnancy with Yasmine and the aftermath of betrayal by infidelity both served as thresholds of pain endured by a 'process" all allowed and designed to bring me closer to God and ultimately witness and win more lost souls for His kingdom. This glitter is gold.

I can't imagine what would be right now if God had other plans written for her, but I know I would have been ready for it either way because the ability to pray had been etched into my mold. I understood the power of prayer early on because I had a praying great-grandmother. God sent Yasmine through me, possibly to change the way we approach pregnancy in teenage and young mothers. I learned how to do my best and allow God to do the rest. I focused on giving her back to God. Just like I did my marriage. When something is not functioning properly, you search for the manufacturer's instructions. You don't throw it away at first sign of malfunction...or dysfunction.

We have made it through almost 18 years, and today, my parenting goal is still to give my children a childhood they won't have to heal from when they become adults. Parenting was challenging for me before it even started. Ideally, you love your children unconditionally and have an idea of how you want their lives to go. However, they are an entire spirit with a unique purpose before even connecting with your flesh in conception. It was super important for me to connect and communicate with God and ask, "who is this person, this spirit you sent through me, and what is their assignment?" Even though I almost gave my power away in destroying her with an abortion, I took it back and made sure I did my part by pressing to maintain a healthy verbal, physical, mental and spiritual environment and atmosphere during my pregnancy. I questioned it then, but now I know God chose me because he knew I could handle it.

God reminded me that in the aftermath of infidelity, this was not the first time I had to rely on what was deposited in my mold. The same way I trusted God with Yasmine was the same was He wanted me to trust Him with Rahsaan and our marriage. I gave my marriage to God the same way I gave him the placenta previa. The same way I gave him the Down's Syndrome diagnosis. The same way I gave him the hole in her heart. The same way I gave him the abortion!

He did it before, he certainly can and will do it again!!

This brings to heart the time David killed Goliath. So many before him had faced Goliath and were killed, forced to join his army, or simply too afraid to try. Then enters David, who knew the value of the prize gained in killing Goliath, stepped up and recalled the times before he faced death while tending the sheep. He said every time a lion or bear attacked a sheep, he killed it. He was confident he would do the same with Goliath, for he said, *"the Lord rescued me from the claws of lions and bears, and he will rescue me from the hands of this Philistine."* It's all in 1 Samuel 17:34-37.

David was positive and confident of victory because of the experiences etched into his mold. You must believe the same God that helped you before is the same God that will help you now.

Let's take it a step further. Once David accepted that God would bring him to victory over Goliath, Saul offered him his armor. David tried it on, but it did not fit. He could barely move. It was too heavy and big. He knew Saul's armor wouldn't work. He resorted to what he knew: his slingshot and rocks!! David put aside Saul's armor and put on the armor intended for him, according to his mold!

Often times when facing trials people around us will offer 'their way' of handling them. And most times it is done in good intention. However, although the trial may be the same, the way we are designed to handle it is different. The grace I receive is different from the grace you receive. The way we handle it has everything to do with our experiences, our molding. I couldn't put on someone else's armor to fight for my marriage. I had to go to the maker of my mold to see what was written for me. If I am created in HIS image and likeness, how then would God handle this? The best and only way to know is to ask.

That pain I felt in my marriage had my mind all jacked up. Once I got out of my own thoughts and got my mind right (battlefield of the mind) everything was clear. I came out of it headfirst...like a baby when it's born. Like giving birth. Birth to myself. My real self. My authentic, bold, unapologetic, never forget who you are again, FREE self!! I saw that those warriors were midwives and coaches, assisting me as I endured through my pain.

There's no baby without pain! No delivery without the contractions. And if you have had a baby, then you know that you push during the contractions. Each one is strategic in assisting you to push what's planted inside of you: a seed to sow and deposit for greatness for the kingdom of God.

Ask God to help you examine your mold. Reflect on the makings of you. See His hand in it all. Search for the glitter from your past that will help you to get through any present trials. Remember God knew you before you were formed. And He knows every decision you will make. He knew Rahsaan would betray me and that I would seek Him to heal and grow me into what He created me to be all along. He knows how to navigate you through whatever you are facing. It is all in your mold.

Part II:

THE *Refining*

ACCORDING TO MERRIAM-WEBSTER: Refining is the process of removing impurities or unwanted elements from (a substance); to bring to a fine or a pure state; free from impurities; to refine metal, sugar, or petroleum.

> *But He knows the way I take (and pays attention to it). When He has tried me, I will come forth as (refined) gold (pure and luminous). Job 23:10 AMP*

When we graduated from high school, I was on my way to Hampton University to pursue a college degree. This was an expectation from my family and not an option. I went on to attend a two-week orientation but ultimately ended up faking sick half-way through the program in order to come home. The truth was I missed Rahsaan. He decided on Morgan State University and was awarded a full band scholarship. I developed extreme anxiety of my future, regarding deciding on a major. For whatever reason, I couldn't imagine a future that was confined within or defined by a degree or title. That mindset made it challenging for me to decide on a program that would shape my next 4 years and beyond. The funny thing about uncertainty is the underlying fear. The fear of what was unknown drove me closer toward my comfort zone instead of pushing me outside of it. And comfort is the enemy of progress. Yet so often we retreat to what we know instead of pushing through the unknown. It's truly a test of faith. Are you willing to walk into a dark room, knowing there is a staircase because God said it, but yet you cannot see it yet? I just couldn't walk through the door. I needed to know all the details of the room, beforehand.

After quitting the program at Hampton, I decided to take a year to 'find myself'. I withdrew from college and enrolled into cosmetology school, where I knew I would be comfortable. I saw it as killing two birds with one stone. I would do something I enjoyed doing and earn a living while doing it. My mother was okay with it because I had a 'plan of action.' My grandfather was a different story. He had a fit, exclaiming, "there is so much more to who you are besides frying black women's hair. You are destined for greater, for higher." And he was right, in part. But I did not understand it then. At the time, his words hurt my feelings. I felt that he didn't believe in me and that I disappointed him with my decision.

Pride came in quickly for me. One dream of mine has always been to be on television, in movies, and in magazines. It did not matter how, I just knew that whatever I did, it would come with some level of good exposure. I enrolled in the full-time cosmetology program at Baltimore Studio of Hair Design located in downtown Baltimore. I started two months after graduating from high school.

Many of my classmates were adults with children and

boyfriends, careers and drama. 'Grown woman drama' is what I called it. It felt like I was that little kid who snuck downstairs to eavesdrop on their mama and her friends' conversations. My life experiences up to that point looked like a Disney movie in comparison. I loved listening to their stories. Stories of success, of heartbreak, of inspiration and of failure. I eventually started to develop a plan for myself. I used my artistic skills and secured a station at a nearby popular nail salon, designing nails with hand paint. One dollar per nail design and five dollars if they wanted diamond-like stones applied or had extra length. I worked three days a week: Monday, Friday, and Saturday, clearing an easy three hundred to five hundred dollars weekly. That was a lot of money for an 18-year-old. I purchased all of the latest material things. Mainly clothes, handbags, and shoes. I often gifted Rahsaan with sneakers, cologne, and a few times, even jewelry. He was a freshman in college without a job then. And I had no problem asking if he wanted to go to The Cheesecake Factory for lunch.

It was a year and half after high school when I became pregnant with our daughter Yasmine. I would do whatever it took to make sure she wanted for nothing. Boy did I have a huge chip on my shoulder. I secured my cosmetologist license and continued with nails until she was old enough for daycare. I went full time with my hair career and cleared 50K my first year in business. That was more than what most of my friends or recent college grads made. Then it hit me. I was bit by the bug. The bug of self-righteousness and pride. I was my own hero.

Rahsaan and I knew we were going to be together forever. He loved playing "Always and Forever" by Earth Wind and Fire. He knew I was his wife and he was my husband. That came with us both eventually taking each other for granted.

At one-point Rahsaan told me "the only thing you need me for now is to bring you lunch". To this day recalling his words make me shake my head in disgust. How did I get to the point of unappreciation with him? The point of making him feel less than valued? I bought my car, had a furnished 2-bedroom apartment and a thriving career. I had traveled out of the state for various hair shows. And I did it with very minimal support from him and no state assistance. I paid my tithes and regularly attended my family's church. Yasmine wanted for nothing. I was living my best! But I was intoxicated with and blinded by "making it happen". I failed to include Rahsaan in 'my plans'. Sometimes I failed to include God too. Don't get me wrong, Rahsaan had his flaws also. He was young, attending parties at nearby colleges and traveling with the band. And then, of course, there were girls. I dealt with a lot from him. He had his faults. Most of which, I chose to overlook. However, it did not take him long to go where he was celebrated and not just tolerated. We broke up, and he ended up seeing another girl shortly after.

I believe this was my first round of refining in the fire.

I knew I was supposed to marry Rahsaan. But how was that going to happen if we were not together? My heartache took its toll on me. One morning I fell to my floor and started crying. Yasmine laid right in front of me and pressed her forehead against mine. Seeing the confusion on her face I got up and pulled myself together. I had never felt that type of rejection before. I made a promise never to allow myself become that messed up over anyone anymore. Especially since my daughter was now watching.

Pray through your process.

God began to show me parts of me that were bringing my value down. The parts that enabled me to put value on the wrong things. The more you go through, the more you are worth. I did not understand that back then. God placed a woman in my life who became a mentor to me. She spoke life into me. She pulled the gracefulness that I had hidden out of me and taught me how to be a woman after God's heart. Her words *"he will want you when you want someone else. Make that someone else is Jesus."* She worked as manager of the hair salon I worked in and shared her wisdom with me by showing me her scars, from her own refining. She was transparent, in that her dust particles and the remnants of glitter sparkled and drew me to her. I knew I could trust her and listen to what she had to share.

The breakup and time apart were painful but also

necessary. The more time I spent with God, the more my heart mended, and my focus changed. It became more about pleasing God than chasing and worshipping other idols. I no longer thought I was better than anyone. I grew wiser with my money. I started mentoring young girls and volunteering my talents at nearby retirement homes, giving elderly women beautiful hairstyles. Eventually, Rahsaan and I decided that we were happier together than apart from each other. Shortly after we started dating each other, again, I was involved in a terrible car accident. A car had run the red light and t-boned my car while I entered the intersection. I was in physical therapy for four months, resulting in Rahsaan moving in with Yasmine and me. By this time, he obtained a full-time job and was able to assist with our living expenses.

How soon did the tables turn?

God can make the person you stepped over while climbing up the ladder, the same person you need help from to stand up on your feet when that ladder breaks. Be careful of who you dismiss. This was the first time I had to submit to depending on Rahsaan...and it wasn't going to be the last time either.

I soon became pregnant with our son. It did not take long playing house for me to know that I was not going to settle for a live-in boyfriend, and so we planned a spring wedding. We were married outdoors and in front of over one hundred guests. Our son was born later that summer. We were in a great space. We started to be clear on the lifestyle we wanted and did whatever it took to get it.

We upgraded everything and dated often. Then Rahsaan started traveling more often for one of our teams in business, resulting in me being a single mother for 4-6 days out of the week. Yet, in those trying times apart we still made each other our priority, being intentional about everything we did together and apart. It made a difference because we conceived our third child unexpectedly. We were on a cloud! He even achieved a promotional milestone in business. It was one that promised a big paycheck in return for big sacrifice. However, we made many mistakes along that journey to his promotion. One being the day after our third child was born, Rahsaan put our business first by attending an event and party while I tended to our newborn alone. 'It's a part of the sacrifice for growth for our business" he said. And I went along with it against my better judgement. I honestly believe it planted a seed of envy and possible competition in me with him. I couldn't wait to get back into the hair salon and have my own time and make my own money. In my mind, he couldn't possibly value me and my sacrifices of giving him children since he chose business over us. I went back to work within 3 weeks after giving birth. I was determined to not ever put myself in that vulnerable place of dependence again. I was disappointed in that one act of his and it brought back arrogance and pride. My career became my focus again. And we were both at what we believed to be the best points of our careers and surprisingly also our marriage and family.

Pray through your process.

We began to fast and started praying for more opened doors. One of those doors carried us to Atlanta, which has always been my ideal place to live and where I could flourish in my career. While packing and preparing for relocation, I found a memory book from high school where I had written inside where I wanted to be in 10 years: married to Rahsaan, living in Atlanta with two or three children, thriving in my career and driving a gold C-class Mercedes Benz. *"As a man thinks so is he"*. My life had become the byproduct of my thoughts and words.

At the same time, Rahsaan suddenly experienced another surge of momentum in his business. Yep. That business. The business I did not initially support because it took most of his time away from us and gave us little to nothing from him in return. The business that I labeled as *'his thing'* because hair was *'my thing'*. The business that required me to sacrifice vacations and hair shows because he had a training event to attend the same weekend and we couldn't do both. The business that I found myself often saying: *"as long as you like it, I love it, but really want no part of it"* about. The business that was not so welcoming to spouses because very few people on the team were married. There I was yet again, praying for clarity and direction. Because his business interfered with my business and usually called for me to put my plans second for the sake of our children. How could this be? I was now married but did not fully understand the meaning of becoming one. Neither of us understood what that meant and entailed.

I had come so far in creating my identity, as a single woman, with goals and dreams. It was hard as ever to introduce that woman to married-with-kids woman I had become. I did not understand what 'dying to myself' truly meant and required. I was finally in the Atlanta where my hairstyling dreams could thrive, and I found myself confused and praying on what to do.

And that's where God said pause.

Pray through your process.

I pressed into Him and received my answer. God led me to Proverbs 31. I asked Him for clarity and He gave me a vision of Rahsaan and I addressing thousands of men and women from a stage. I couldn't tell what we were doing exactly or what we were attending, but we were speaking. And we were a united front.

I was sitting with the very thing I wanted most right in front of me. I truly wanted God's plans for my life more than anything, but my flesh was struggling. God gave me a glimpse of the kind of woman He whispered into existence in me, the kind of wife he created me to be and the wife he intended for Rahsaan. Everything I thought I knew, I had to learn differently.

"I was called to be his wife. It was my destiny to stand beside him." ~ Coretta Scott King.

God brought the graceful Coretta Scott King back into my spirit. A few years prior, I studied her life. I was drawn to her and often wondered how she did it. Now, Rahsaan is not Martin Luther King, Jr. He is, however, chosen to do a mighty thing for God's kingdom. In an interview before her death, Coretta Scott King shared, *"What most did not understand then, was that I was not only married to the man I loved, but I was also married to the movement that I loved... I didn't marry a man; I married a destiny."* That resonated in my spirit when I heard it! God showed me part of Rahsaan's destiny. He showed me my connection to it. I know Rahsaan will step into it in God's timing.

Whatever God calls your husband towards, he also calls you towards. There IS power in your partnership.

Over two years I was refined. God revealed to me that I lacked trust. In people, because I was guarded instead of trusting my discernment. I lacked trust in Rahsaan, because I feared letting him lead us. And ultimately, I lacked trust in God himself, because I constantly had a "make it happen mindset," not pushing myself to get out of the way and rather rely on His will.

God supplies all of our needs according to HIS riches and glory. He had a plan for me, to prosper me and not fail me, one of hope and a future. I was in the fire to refine my patience. My lack of patience rushed things before their time. Resulting in me then begging God to fix it. During those two years I learned how to truly pray, in depth and not just length.

Over time I developed a Proverbs 31:10-31 spirit. I served my family and spoke vision into my husband's business affairs. I prayed, God revealed it, I spoke it, Rahsaan received it, and it came into manifestation. Things were great. We had a beautiful home, his business was thriving, and we were happy. We were very happy. We finally felt like we had come to the light at the end of the tunnel. I started attending events with him. I knew who I was and who I was becoming. I stepped into MY position. God carved out a lane just for me. One that had room for me to love God, support my husband and pour into him, as well as other women and ultimately our team. Refinement brought all of the damaging stuff to the surface, and God skimmed it right off: the attitude, the pride, the division and confusion.

I should have known something was coming my way. Comfort is the enemy of progress.

One evening, a close friend asked me about a woman business partner of my husband's. This business partner was someone I went to elementary school with yet did not maintain a connection with over the decades, until later reconnecting on social media. Upon reconnecting, she shared with me her desire to change her family's financial tree, to retire herself and her husband and to spend more time with their children. From afar, the business partner appeared to be a happy and devoted wife. With the intent of being supportive to her growth in business, I agreed with having Rahsaan to travel back and forth to Baltimore to help her build her organization. Why not? There was absolutely no inclination that this was a bad idea since I didn't have the stress of working and finding childcare while he was gone, as I did in the past. Also she was super friendly and accommodating to the fact that my husband took time away from his wife and children to help her family. We ended the year on a high note, with our goals, as well as goals for our team in tow.

Things were great as far as I was concerned. I thought his travel would slow down once our baby was born, but I was wrong. Something changed and I can't pinpoint when. I remember the day like it was yesterday, seeing him hold our fresh out of the womb baby in his arms while gazing into her eyes and have that moment interrupted by a text message he received. He read it and said 'I have to travel back to Baltimore. The team needs me and she's almost near her promotion." There we were again, like 'déjà vu', and I remembered how I felt the last time I gave birth and fought to voice it to him. Instead I ignored my thoughts and feelings. I ignored the fact that I had just given birth and deep down inside I wanted my husband to bring his newborn home and for us not to be apart as we had done in the past. But the nature of our business had become 'sacrifice now for reward later'. Rahsaan was so convinced that passing that small, but symbolic act off to someone else on our support team was well worth the exchange and sacrifice. So, I obliged...yet again. He continued, back and forth to Baltimore to help her. Not too far later, the questions started coming my way from my friends about her: *"what's up with her?"* *"what's going on with them?"* *"she's talking about him like they're close."* *"why doesn't she like you?"* There were so many questions! It was if I carried a weight in my stomach every time someone mentioned her name. And I just didn't know what it was!

I felt something different. Something very different.

What I perceived as "instinct" was really the whispers of the Holy Spirit. I had to learn to trust Him, to listen to Him, to believe Him. One thing I didn't do right away was to trust what I felt. I argued with it constantly, going back and forth with myself. It was because my eyes showed me one thing, but my spirit told something totally different. And I did not want to listen to it. So, I did what most wives do...or perhaps should do. I prayed and told God that I trust him and, in his time, he will reveal what I need to know and what I can handle. I told myself this even when I didn't fully believe it. I had to, so I could move forward. If there was anything for me to discover or 'catch', I knew that God would show me in a way only he knew I would receive. I was so confused by what I felt in my spirit, which contradicted what I saw with my natural eyes. I couldn't figure it out. Not to forget, I was caring for a new baby, battling with post-partum depression as well!

So, I prayed and fought spiritually.

There were times in which the other woman would say something, and randomly throw a dig at me or slick comment out to see if I'd react and I had to bite my tongue every time. I had to give it to God.

Spiritual warfare is real! Believe that with everything.

There are quarterly conferences held every year in our business and depending on what was happening with our children, I sometimes accompanied Rahsaan to them. I enjoyed seeing business partners from other states and sneaking some "me time" away from home. We attended the first one of the new year, which happened to fall a few weeks after our last child was born. I was also dealing with an unknown bleeding disorder and was going into week nine of hemorrhaging. I was physically, spiritually, emotionally, and mentally weak. I saw our business partner, the other woman for the first time since the last conference and giving birth, and it was very strange. She said something weird about Rahsaan in earshot of those in the vicinity, and he acted as if it was nothing. I wanted to confront her so bad and curse her out in the lobby. I wanted to hear what she said. I had to remind myself that any issue, if any will be with my husband and not her. My flesh was on fire and I couldn't tell if it was because I was annoyed by her actions or mad at him for being so nonchalant about them. That brief encounter left me holed up in my hotel room with welts that later appeared on my face. It looked as if someone or something with claws had scratched both sides of my face from behind. I missed our team dinner because I looked like I was in a fight. I still remember the sting that my tears caused, running over them. That was the point I knew I was at war. At war with something demonic. Something angry, hurt, and vengeful. Something that absolutely hated marriage and the power that comes from two people joined together by God.

We drove home from the conference in near silence. When we arrived home, I grilled him with questions. It was the first time I asked him if he was sleeping with her and he looked me dead in my eyes and said "no". She actually called me too. And during that conversation she called me "trophy wife" for the first time. It felt like I had entered the Twilight Zone. The more Rahsaan traveled to Baltimore, the more our lifestyle crumbled. Our business began to suffer, bills were piling up, I was passing out from blood loss ending up in the emergency room for blood transfusions, we experienced a repossession and were facing eviction. Our life did a 180-degree turn. We made the painful decision to move back to Baltimore, for many reasons but for me, to have my husband home in our bed every night. I lost so much weight that year. On top of that, it was difficult for me to work because I kept getting sick. I went through the humility of having to apply for food stamps and energy assistance for the first time, praying no one saw me in the social services office. We needed all the financial help we could get. And one of our daughters had a seizure. Rahsaan froze when it happened and completely broke down, providing no support at all. I had never experienced so much at once in all areas of my life...ever. And all of this going on behind the scenes while having to smile for our team keeping face for the position we held and worst of all be around this other woman not knowing my husband was having an affair with her. Those summer months were the hardest ever. I kept asking God what we did to deserve storm after storm. Praying for a breakthrough and restoration in my health. Smiling through tears when I received small moments of joy. Our date nights stopped, and I was miserable.

I was finally cleared to return to work fall of that same year, so I hit the pavement running. I was determined to get back to me, since I felt that I lost myself in the midst of adjusting to my new normal of four children while overcoming thinking that we've failed for moving back to Baltimore, and feeling like a fraud to our team for losing all that we lost. I was done with isolating myself and fighting alone.

A few weeks into getting my rhythm back, I sat at the dryer while waiting for my next client to arrive. It's something about the white noise the dryer makes that gave me stillness. I asked God to give me something, someone to trust. I mentioned in prayer that it felt like a demon was trying to take me out. I felt its presence so heavy whenever I was around this other woman, but I honestly didn't know how to fight it. God showed up that day. I had become so paranoid of social media because over the summer, a mutual acquaintance reached out to me pleading to talk. This person shared with me that this other woman intentionally befriended people I was connected to online to get a closer view to me. The messenger advised me to be careful. As this other woman watches my every move. And from that, I distanced myself from social media. However, that day I sat at the dryer in the salon, I heard the Holy Spirit say the answer is there on social media. Facebook to be exact. I logged on and the very first post on my newsfeed came from a locally DMV-area known prophetess. Prior to this day I had no direct interaction with her. In the Facebook post, she spoke about Jesus cleansing the man of the unclean spirits. It took everything in me to reach out to her. I was desperate and needed help. I needed someone to believe me, to listen to me, to empathize with me. I explained everything I had been hearing and seeing throughout the year and in my home, asking her if it was possible for a person to latch onto another person's life. Her immediate response confirmed that I was at war with the Jezebel spirit. The Jezebel spirit comes from Queen Jezebel who is in the Old Testament of the Bible. She is known for manipulating and killing many of God's prophets. The Jezebel spirit is very cunning, seductive, and controlling. It shows up in multiple ways. The prophetess told me to immediately cut off communication with the other woman and that she would be in touch. It took her four days, but she came through for me.

Early on in my life I learned that my hands are gifted. They are considered anointed. I saw hair growth in areas that had become completely bald. When we are born again Christian and receive the Holy Spirit, we also receive a spiritual gift. These gifts include increased faith, the word of wisdom, the word of knowledge, the gifts of healing, the gifts of miracles, discernment of spirits, prophecy, speaking of tongues, and interpretation of tongues. The purpose of these gifts is to build the body of the entire Church. Because I know that my hands are gifted, I also believe I have the gift of healing through the act of laying on of hands. It all connected for me when the prophetess instructed me to get oil and taught me how to anoint it. She explained that the only way to fight was with the word of God and to physically touch by laying of my hands on and anoint everything, EVERYTHING that my husband touched and that touched him. So that is what I did. I anointed my hands with oil, and I prayed! I laid hands on Rahsaan's head while he slept. I touched all his clothes hanging in our closet, his shoes, belts, even his underwear and socks! I touched and prayed over his keys, the steering wheel in his car, his laptop and iPad. Everything. Then I went through our home, touching the doorknobs and windows.

She told me to pray the other woman "away" as well. I cleansed my body and prayed that my *"fragrance"* would overtake him when we made love. Which was another direct instruction from her: not to refuse sex, as it is mentioned in 1 Corinthians 7:5 (NKJV) :"*Do not deprive one another except with consent for a time, that you may give yourselves to fasting and prayer; and come together again so that Satan does not tempt you because of your lack.*" I prayed that he would recognize my scent. It was work. A lot of work. She said to rest and trust God, and that all I needed to know will rear its head when I need to know it. I can honestly say that I felt peace for the first time in a very long time after that. I smiled every time I came around our team and business events, did my best to remain as graceful as possible.

When you understand who you are becoming in Christ, who you are selected and chosen to be, you also understand that you don't have to fight or compete for anything. There's no competition. There's no need to belittle or attack anyone. The battle is already won. You just have to step into victory.

I was in the fire again. Being still, so that my flesh would die. So that I wouldn't react in a moment of rage or lose my mind and cause a scene that would hurt us all. Rahsaan never gave me any reason not to trust him. I wasn't some mystery locked away in a tower for his eyes only. He celebrated me. He loved on me. I had no 'hard' evidence of infidelity. Just hearsay. Her husband stopped coming around, suddenly. He must've sensed something too. I confronted Rahsaan about the rumors and again he denied them. I wasn't in the business of sneaking around, looking for stuff. We didn't have that type of relationship. We didn't have each other's passwords or codes. We never had reason to request them or use them.

On the contrary, it was her who made me uncomfortable, and made others raise an eyebrow. She was being used by the devil to bring strife, division and confusion into my life. Into our business. Into our purpose. She was broken and not whole. Rahsaan chose and welcomed all of this. Maybe to mask his brokenness. Maybe to escape from reality. I don't place blame on her, or even Satan for that matter, for he can't operate without willing participants. Rahsaan made a promise to me in our vows, not her. Rahsaan decided, every time, regardless of what it was doing to me and to us. Whew! Thank God for grace!

Jesus says in the first part of John 10:10 *"The thief comes only to steal and kill and destroy."*

Steal.

Kill.

Destroy.

Recognize when the enemy shows up.

The devil fears you realizing your power and discovering your purpose. He fears you going after it and getting everything that God has for you! Recognize the enemy and call him out! But don't stop there, you must also get to the place of casting them out, resisting the devil and watching him flee! Demons tremble at the sound of Jesus' name! Call them out!!!

> *It was hard but I had to learn to pray and push through the process.*

I was in the middle of a fight that I didn't even fully know I was in. Struggling every day with what I believed and felt in my spirit. I had to continue to trust God. The work He had started in me was worth it. It was not an option to throw in the towel. I wasn't going to compromise this fight. I won't paint this picture that I held it entirely together. I didn't trust anyone. In public, I held my tongue and kept my head held high. But in private, I poured out my heart to God through my journal:

August 20th

"I'm tired of wrestling with my thoughts. Something has entered my home and it's draining my spirit. I'm sick most of the time, happy some of the time, and paranoid at other times. People keep telling me of their suspicion of infidelity. I have zero proof. What is happening? I feel like I'm being watched. People are looking at me like I'm insane. What is he saying about me? What is happening when I'm not there? Do people see something and not want to be upfront with me? If I say something and it isn't true it might put a strain on our business. It may drive people away. There's been a transferal of energy..."

Then immediately, in the same entry, I wrote:

"Lord I trust you. This hurts very badly. If he is sleeping with another man's wife, he cursed himself. He cursed our family. We're losing everything. I won't lose my faith. Please show me what's in my heart. Take these thoughts. Replace them with your thoughts. Remind me who I am. I am more than a conqueror. I am fearfully and wonderfully made. I am set apart. Perhaps I was born for such a time as this. Blessed is she who believes what The Lord has promised. You promised me a faithful, loving husband who honors me and glorifies your name. I'm in the fire, but I won't smell like smoke. You said beauty for my ashes. Hold your head up queen. Everything set up against my health, my marriage, my family, career, and business is defeated in the name of Jesus. God is doing something new in me. I feel the urge to go off, but my heart won't let me. He will keep in perfect peace he whose mind stays on him. Help me stay focused on you, Lord. Focus on Jesus Erica."

Refining is an ongoing process. With a new level comes a refining. The unwanted spiritual elements in you don't have room or access to where God is taking you. And so, it must be purged out. It's done in our trials.

You are like a piece of gold.
You ARE gold.

Gold in its raw form is really a rock, amongst all the dirt. And it's found in the depths of the earth. Its hard to see the hidden potential of what is underneath the dirt.

But God sees it all differently. He finds us in the raw form and sees our hidden potential. He refines us in the fire and gets us pure. And a fact about gold is the longer it's left in the fire, the higher its value becomes. And the more you go through, the more you are worth!

That was me. *I prayed and pressed through the process.*

I was no longer surprised at the *"fiery ordeal, which was taking place to test me, to test the quality of my faith, as though something strange or unusual was happening to me (1 Peter 4:12)."* The bible says *"these trials will show that your faith is genuine. It is being tested as fire tests and purifies gold, though your faith is more precious than gold. So, when your faith remains strong enough through many trials, it will bring you much praise and glory and honor on the day when Jesus Christ is revealed to the whole world. (1 Peter 1:7)"*

My peace came in knowing and believing what Paul said in 1 Corinthians 10:13: *"you are tempted in the same way that everyone else is tempted. But God can be trusted to not let you be tempted too much, and he will show you how to escape from your temptations."*

Amen!

Want to know how to overcome spiritual warfare and attacks? Pray and listen to God. I believe He puts just enough on us to apply pressure to seek Him. Enough to break us for His glory and purpose in the Earth. Because if we could get through it without him, then we wouldn't need him. He knows the way. Seek Him. Name those spirits, rebuke them and watch them tremble and flee! Don't operate in an old revelation of yesterday. Overcoming spiritual warfare requires us to walk in a right now revelation, listening and heeding to every command of the Holy Spirit. It also requires fasting. Diligent and intentional fasting allows you to die of your flesh so that the new can be sustained. All your experiences and trauma are absorbed into the molecular structure of your cells. Fast and turn those cells over for new ones. Purge your 'shell' so that your spirit will thrive and respond accordingly. You have work to do. Fasting brings clarity. This work can't be done through dirty lenses and a sluggish body that constantly falls into the old patterns of muscle memory.

I had been molded, then refined, and refined again, and again. The spirits in me and around me in others that warred against the me, had been pressed and burned and washed out. I had a renewed mind. One that was also ready to be renewed and restored in my marriage.

That right time that the prophetess spoke about showed up, just as she said: when I was ready for it.

Part III:

THE *Polishing*

ACCORDING TO MERRIAM-WEBSTER, Polishing is the process of creating a smooth and shiny surface by rubbing it or using a chemical action, leaving a surface with a significant specular reflection.

It is written in Romans 8:17, that we are joint heirs with Christ, *"if indeed we suffer with Him, that we may also be glorified together."* Therefore, let us, *"consider that the sufferings of this present time are not worthy to be compared with the glory which shall be revealed in us (Romans 8:18)."* You can't be polished without friction.

A new year had turned. Things slowed down in her business as far as my interaction and engagement was concerned and Rahsaan had placed his focus on other things including home. I guess he was tired of covering up his lies. And at this point, we had pretty much lost everything. I decided to breathe fresh air into our life and attended the first regional event of the new year for our business. So many familiar faces greeted me with welcome arms, expressing that they had missed me and were glad I had come back around. What occurred next was nothing but God. Remember when I said I made peace with knowing that God would reveal what I needed to know how He knew I would receive it? Well I ran into a dear friend from New York while on the lunch break during the event. She pulled me to the side and said "I have something important to tell you. I've been praying for you without ceasing. There is a woman..." I immediately felt my stomach drop when she said that because I knew where she was going. I hadn't spoken to her in over a year and I hadn't been around anyone for her to know anything. She went on to explain that she had a dream and it involved Rahsaan and another woman, but not to be deceived by this other woman's actions. To understand that this has everything to do with Rahsaan and I and less about this other woman. She held my hands and started praying for me. All I could do was cry, standing in the middle of a busy food court. I didn't care who saw me. I released a pain that I didn't know I still had. And this is still without hard proof of any infidelities. She ended our encounter with "trust God. Rahsaan has lost himself, caught up in a mess and the grip is tight, so don't ask him anything or listen to anything he says. Fight the spirit, not the person. Your prayers are heard and answered. Trust God."

The ride home was quiet...again. Rahsaan asked me if I was ok because someone else saw me crying and told him. I couldn't even talk to him. I didn't want to hear him lie again. I just couldn't take it anymore. I guess my holding all I wanted to say to him had an adverse effect on me because I ended up hemorrhaging uncontrollably and ended up back in the emergency room for another blood transfusion. However, this time was different. I had a new doctor who decided to try a new treatment on me.

My doctor was hopeful and the next day I went home to restricted bedrest. Almost a week later in the middle of the night I started bleeding again. I crawled my way to our bathroom which was in our bedroom. Without wanting to wake up the household, I called for Rahsaan who was right in bed outside of the door but to no avail he wouldn't wake up. Everything about this was by grand design. Remember I mentioned how we never ever checked each other's phones? While leaving the bathroom to get back in bed, his cellphone lit up. This is the same man who always powered his phone off at night, and suddenly it's lighting up from a message notification at 3-something in the morning. I was tempted for the first time to go through his phone. "Resist it Erica, don't you do it." I repeated to myself as I passed his side of the bed to get to mine. Once it lit up two more times I couldn't resist! I opened his phone and there they were, pictures of her in a matching bra and panty set! They were accompanied by a simple "I miss you" text message. I scrolled through the message thread, noticing breaks in the dates. The most current one had a two-month break in communication. And they were clear and concise, some from her saying how she missed him to which sometimes he'd respond, "leave me alone" or "I love my wife" or worse "meet me" and "what are you doing?" I would have probably never seen them if I went through his phone any other time because he used a texting app that hid the messages.

I felt a feeling I'm embarrassed to say I felt. I wanted

to kill him. I felt rage. I felt a pain in my chest. I felt grief. The kind I imagine I would feel if I mourned death. It is indescribable. Therefore, I can't question why people do what they do, because moments of passion and rage are real, and hard to ration through in the moment. My body got hot and I woke him up by throwing the phone at him.

Most of that night is a blur. However, Rahsaan said it was the one and only time he ever felt the physical manifestation of my rage and knew I was hurt. He held me to stop me from hitting him and can you believe he immediately confessed and owned his mess?

Those piercing words "you're just a trophy wife" came to mind from my stomach on up, and they tasted like vomit. Those words fit perfectly into the messed-up puzzle I had been trying to put together since that cold day at the quarterly conference the previous year. It brought the picture together to make sense for me. But what didn't make sense was why.

Once the cat was out of the bag, all lies uncovered and secrets revealed, I was faced with yet another trial. Where do we go from here? I no longer recognized him. I no longer recognized myself. We had to find our way back to each other and become one, again. And I had to find myself, again.

Polishing involves vigorous rubbing. Almost as if you are wiping something off. I had to go deeper spiritually to scrub my mind of the image I had of myself. An image of a tainted wife. I felt a sense of betrayal to myself for choosing us instead of me. I had to forgive myself. Which required a lot of time in the mirror, reflecting inward and asking God what else is there inside, that is reflecting on the outside and needs to be polished? This also included counseling and therapy. A lot of it. I don't why so many are against counseling, but it changed my life. Go to therapy!

I hit rock bottom.

When we confront that which is within, good and bad, we learn our truth. And when we keep what is necessary for our purpose and release what no longer serves it, we are whole, and we shine! This polishing process was me, allowing God's image to now reflect on myself as well as my marriage. Forgiveness and trust are two of the most essential ingredients during this process. As I was learning how to trust Rahsaan, I was also learning how to trust myself. How to truly embrace forgiveness. How to believe again. How to believe in us again.

What is forgiveness?

Searching Google Dictionary, I found that Forgiveness is the action or process of forgiving or being forgiven. To forgive is to stop feeling angry or resentful toward (someone) for an offense, flaw, or mistake.

Why is it so hard to forgive?

It's like the world pushes reconciliation before forgiveness. Most would rather be concerned with what it looks like than what it is. So, when you forgive someone, especially if in my case a spouse who stepped outside of marriage, it is easy to feel urged to reconcile quickly. I encourage you to forgive first, then allow the relationship to organically come back together.

And I know some are reading this thinking: But Erica, how could you get over *this*? How could you get over this *huge* mountain in your marriage? The disappointment... THAT betrayal... the distrust... and then move forward in trust, love, AND forgiveness?

How do you do that when it hurts so bad and the resentment still brings a bitter taste in my mouth...

Oftentimes wives will talk to others about their mountains and whether they need to press into prayer. To pray for their husbands. For their marriages. For their peace AND themselves. And oftentimes the very next thing they think is, *"I'm so mad at him that I can't pray for him...why does he deserve that from me?"*

The anger I felt for my husband, the overwhelming hurt and disappointment made it extremely difficult for me to pray. I remember sitting in a corner on the floor pleading with God to remove it so I could pray. I asked God to remove how I saw my husband and to show me how He saw him. How I saw Rahsaan made me feel like he didn't deserve anything from me. I had to fight to see my husband how God saw him. And God reminded me that my husband was also His creation and child.

There it was.

Since I know that my husband is a child of God, and that God even commands us to love and pray for our enemies...who am I really to tell God no if He asked me to pray for my husband? Taking the focus off my feelings and placing them on the truth and Word of God made it easier for me to forgive and pray for him.

Before he was my husband, their father, their leader or friend...and before he was that business owner or even employee, all roles with responsibilities and titles, he IS a child of God. And so, I prayed. I prayed for him and I prayed for myself. I prayed for my marriage. And forgive.

And one of the first things to do in order to truly forgive is to identify the root. Identify any more lingering strongholds. Identify the triggers and acknowledge the pain. God can't heal what we won't reveal. Be honest.

The truth was my husband hurt me.

I also had to forget. Yep, forget. I rewrote the narrative. Otherwise I would replay it over and over in your head reliving the pain each time. I healed because I chose to. Because I wanted to. I let it go. Just. Like. That. It was not and is not an overnight thing. Rather, I became very familiar with *"I'm not okay, but I will be okay"* because I needed to be truthful. Speaking truth allows you to take back your power.

I also learned to be okay with not receiving an apology.

I mentioned that Rahsaan apologized. I saw his remorse up close. She, on the other hand, wasn't genuine and denied everything. She offered up a dry *"I apologize IF..."* that came after I exchanged some hurtful words with her.

The truth was that I didn't need her apology. I ultimately forgave her without it. Forgiveness was for *MY* own sake and sanity. Not theirs. I got to choose to forgive and to forget. Remembering what happened is a self-defense mechanism. We think that if we never forget it then we will never allow it to happen again, because we will recognize it and cut it off before it has a chance to offend us again. And that mechanism is one of fear.

I had to put fear aside, and rather learn and see the lesson of what God wants to manifest through what took place. Otherwise I knew that He would continue to get my attention by any means that He pre-qualifies.

Polishing is literally the act of being in God's hands while he shines you up!

Polishing involves true self-care. And what exactly is self-care? What does it look like? It has become a social media trend now to preach about self-care while promoting cute products and nice services to go along with it. But not many suggestions or steps for true self-care. It isn't just spa days or taking a trip or even enjoying a glass of wine with a bubble bath. Those things can contribute to our happiness and relaxation. And they are great additions. However, I'm not talking about surface-care. I'm talking about authentic self-care, or better yet soul-care which isn't cute and pretty. It starts out ugly and evolves into beautiful.

Soul-care also includes addressing the deep-down hidden-inside hurts that you've buried. Or even carried inside passed on from generations before you. *AHA* I broke a generational curse!! Marriage has been broken with my parents and very scarce on my paternal side of my family.

It's addressing those things that happened way before your existence yet have a very present influence on how you react and respond to emotional trauma. It's also about addressing what maintains your peace and creating a healthy balance of that. It's about the content of your conversations, the shows you watch, music you listen to, books you read, people you're around...activities you engage in to fill a void...It's about being loyal to your emotional bank and setting boundaries, from anything that compromises it. It's about honesty. It's about not being afraid to say *"I don't like something or someone's energy"* and then taking action to remove yourself from it...

You were somebody before you became their mommy or his wife or both, at the same time in some cases. That person matters. *SHE* matters. So, for starts, buy that dress. Get that massage and facial. Schedule that brunch or sister-friend outing. Read that book. Listen to that podcast. Take that vacation. Take a long bubble bath... with a glass of wine if you prefer. Take that class. Do what you love and feel good about yourself. Without explanation.

Soul-care is also about therapy and counseling.

Therapy. And. Counseling.

Whew. That is a mouth full by itself and a lot to unpack and digest.

I saw a therapist. My therapist was more like a spiritual midwife. She was a supporting cast member in *the rebirth of Erica Grier*. She helped me go back generations of my existence. To see how I took on the burden of the *"strong black woman,"* not allowing myself the space to process things and heal. To see how watching my mother run from her hurt, looking for relief in the wrong people, places, and things, was toxic and absolutely not healthy. I had to confront and deal with how I learned how to process pain while in my childhood. And then I learned how to release it, making room for the healing balm from God to renew and restore.

There are generations of ideas, concepts, and beliefs that have been pressed into our fibers. Ideas of the woman as the pillar of strength, taking care of our families, serving in our churches, keeping our communities together, all while still looking good and kept together physically in shape. Meanwhile, that woman might be slowly dying inside due to the stress of not ever taking the time to process, relate, then release what has happened to her. Many do not speak about taking the time to replenish their

The *Polishing* 77

mental, emotional, and spiritual cups. And how to keep it full, giving only the overflow to everyone and everything she serves.

And when you add infidelity! This may be shocking but many replied saying *"that's nothing your grandmother didn't go through..."* *"every woman has had to deal with it..."* or *"get over it."*

I refused to have something that looked good but was rotting and crippling on the inside.

I won.

And so have you!

I told myself: *"I have to be polished so that my grandchildren won't battle what I didn't heal!!!! Mommy didn't get it right, but I will. Daddy didn't get it right, but I will! Generational blessings will overtake my life!!! What giant am I going to kill in my generation so that my kids won't have to in theirs? I don't want my kids fighting the same ones I did."*

I confronted it all and let God polish it up!

Allow God to polish you and reflect who He says you are. You are gold! You are a Queen! You are a Princess! You are Royalty! A joint heir to the throne, in the kingdom of God and on Earth!

The polishing is a journey of recovery and restoration to take back everything the enemy tried to steal from us. There's residue from sin, the memories. The enemy is afraid of us becoming whole. If you know who you are you don't take things that are less than what you deserve. You only accept what is yours.

The Polishing stage, for me, was about building my relationship with Jesus...going higher and deeper into another realm.

God sees our brokenness in the polishing and smooths and shines it right on up, through revealing and healing. The worst in us does not define us. Remember, *ALL* things work together for the good of them who love God and are called according to *HIS* purposes!

What are some ways you take care of yourself? Your mental care? Your emotional care? Your spiritual care? Identify them and write them down. Keep them close by and apply them.

Polishing pushed me to confront the very thing that opened my eyes to there being something going on in the first place: her words *"you're just his trophy wife."* WORDS HOLD POWER. She tried to define me by a title, and I let her. It became easier for her to judge me and justify their actions, as well as ultimately deny them. I had to ask God what was it that *HE* wanted me to do with them. I had to take my power back from them and use them as weapons. Weapons to unify and not divide and judge.

Instead of hitting rewind, I simply pressed delete. I forgave and decided to forget.

I later found out from my husband that her *"Trophy Wife"* disrespect came from a picture he posted of me on his Facebook page. I was 9 months pregnant, glowing, and beautiful in his sight. He snapped a pic of me and uploaded it. He hashtagged #trophywife, I guess because he was proud. These were words from a moment of gratitude, adoration and love, captured and shared. A proud husband saying 'my beautiful wife' was hijacked by the enemy and used as artillery.

Let God buff out those blemishes, otherwise known as bad memories.

And Trust.

I grew to trust God again. I believed what He said and knew I had to also learn to trust my husband again. And I had to let go of my insecurity and be vulnerable again. Insecurity is a form of pride. As I was being insecure, I was basically viewing myself with so much importance, that I lost sight of God.

The more God polished, the more my reflection became His. I also saw that my lack of trust was a form of idol worshipping. 1 Corinthians 13:5 says that love *"keeps no record of wrongs,"* then goes on to say, *in verse seven that love "always protects, always trusts, always hopes, always perseveres."* His will for our lives will never contradict the His word. So, when we are distrusting of our spouse, or anyone for that matter, we are still idolizing them by putting so much importance on their actions; thereby allowing their thinking and actions to affect our feelings. I had to turn to Christ for healing and to fill me up with that supernatural love, which would allow me to forgive, wipe the slate clean, and change my thinking so I could trust again. And then, I prayed that the Holy Spirit changed my husband and filled him with the self-control, the inner-dominion necessary to make the right decisions.

All the blemishes were being rubbed away because I was no longer hiding them. He was buffing out the blemishes.

Remember I said I hit rock bottom?

I had to release the pain and get back to me. Back to what made me happy. I sat with myself and asked what activities did I enjoy doing? What were some of my favorite things? In order to answer these questions, I had to write out a list. Every time I released something painful, I had to think of something that I loved that made me happy to replace the pain with. I drew a blank many times. But I didn't get discouraged. I wanted to be free, more than anything. For days, I only had one thing on my list. And it was the color gold. Strange, I know. But it's the truth. Seeing gold made me smile. It warmed me up inside. I made it a priority to get some things that were gold. The pen I started writing this book with was gold. The planner I purchased was shiny metallic gold. About a week or so later my list began to expand.

> *Take some time out of your day and build on your happy list. *

The more I shared our testimony and my truth, the more God polished and shined me up. We found that we were not alone. That many go through this in their marriage, yet only a few remain married. Even fewer are happy and thriving. And hardly no one talks about it openly.

The polishing process brought out another old blemish that needed to be smoothed out. One morning, soon after Rahsaan became discouraged in his business and asked me to work with him again. I tried to get there. To that place where I could speak life into his dream and pour out encouragement. I tried listening to weekly training calls. And it was also the same day I decided to commit to singing and serving on our church's choir ministry. We were sharing one vehicle at the time, so we had to choose which was most important since once again our commitments collided. And of course, once again, he won. I cried and vented most of that morning. I hardly said two words to him before he left and into the entire day. Now, this is years after his infidelity and we were good, back on Happy Street at the corner of One-Accord Way. I couldn't understand why I felt the resentment and irritation the way I did. A few weeks later, I finally heard my answer: *The beginning of conversion is irritation! The thing that irritates you, is sometimes the thing that changes you.*

I woke up with some clarity after that revelation. I realized that our business had been my enemy because it represents a loss for me. When it came into our life, I opposed it out of fear or losing time in relationship and of sacrifice of my career. At a time in my prime, where my dreams were clear and manifesting, it entered and seemed to steal. I completely missed the possibility that God sent us the business, so that we would learn how to operate at high capacity to serve *HIS* people *TOGETHER*.

Polishing served as a mirror, reflecting me back to me! I saw!! I confronted! And I healed, as He shined me up!

Get in position! Get polished! Embrace it!

The Holy Spirit said, *"Where God has called your husband, he also calls you."* I had limited God and where He's called us. I limited our potential. I resented the *business instead of allowing it to let us become a UNIT of ONE,* in marriage, working together and being an example of a Godly marriage and partnership for many.

That morning I realized and heard and owned a truth that I didn't realize was even a truth: I didn't truly love our business and I didn't love it because it revealed a fear in me. And that fear manifested in infidelity and shortcoming on my behalf. I repented and allowed God to show me what is truth and what is false. I confronted our business and had a real heart to heart conversation (literally conversing as if our business sat at the opposite side of a table from me) with the truths, its purpose in my life, as well as my purpose in it.

What are you resenting or have a love/hate relationship with? What's irritating and causing you friction? Reveal it in the reflection of the polishing. What I heard during my meditation was: *"my daughter *laughter* I sent this to train you both, to teach you how to move as a unit, how to connect with people. To develop your people skills. I sent you as sheep amongst wolves, to fight and be prepared for the next level I've prepared for you. Embrace what I told you. Embrace what I showed you. Embrace it! You are sheep amongst wolves!"* I made peace with our business. For once and for all.

> *Stay alert. This is hazardous work I'm assigning you. You're going to be like sheep running through a wolf pack, so don't call attention to yourselves. Be as cunning as a snake, inoffensive as a dove. Don't be naive. Some people will impugn your motives, others will smear your reputation – just because you believe in me. Don't be upset when they haul you before the civil authorities. Without knowing it, they've done you – and me – a favor, given you a platform for preaching the kingdom news! And don't worry about what you'll say or how you'll say it. The right words will be there; the Spirit of your Father will supply the words. Matthew 10:16-20 MSG*

You have been set apart and placed here for purpose, for kingdom assignment and building, you have *Godfidence*! You reflect His image of you!

After my tears dried, I eventually apologized to Rahsaan, again, and repented to God. I apologized for abandoning him. For not fully trusting his vision for our family and ultimately leaving him to fight alone. I am happy to say that I serve with joy alongside my husband, helping him build, speaking when God tells me and being an example to others.

Never again would I allow anyone to define me. And neither should you! God knew you and I before He formed us in our mothers' wombs. Remember, He has great plans for us. I no longer give my power away. What is inside of me, the world did not put it there so the world cannot take it out. I'm free from opinion and criticism. Treat life and lessons like sandpaper and allow them to polish you! The ultimate purpose of being polished is to live a righteous/holiness life for God, reflecting Christ with your people skills and being an inspiration to God's children both the lost and found.

> *When you refuse to embrace the lessons of your youth you rob your womanhood of the confidence and wisdom that makes your journey beautiful. Your skin is tough because it's made of gold. Don't let life dull your shine. - Sarah Jakes Roberts*

Now you're ready! Right?

No?

There's something else?

Yes, there's something else.

This leads me to the final part of making a trophy. It's the smallest part yet the absolute most important one. While writing this book, initially it had three parts: The Molding, The Refining, and The Polishing. For days I prayed, asking God to give me the creative space to be free and write. As I was going over the outline with Rahsaan, thinking he wasn't listening, he sat straight up and spoke. He is very cautious and intentional with his words so I knew whatever he had to say would be good. He asked *"Erica, what's the one thing people ask us the most?"* I pondered and then it hit me! People often ask: *"How do we make it work? How do we make it last so long?"* The answer is simple: we want to. Our will to last is there. It is something that can't be seen but felt. It's felt in our intentions. We are intentional about our love and wellness.

But our will is also connected to God's will. His will is not seen by the naked eye, but by the Spirit. And it is revealed in our intent to love, honor, and respect each other. I/We have a new foundation (faith), that we are mounted on by a screw (will) that holds us all together.

Part IV:

THE *Mounting*

ACCORDING TO MERRIAM-WEBSTER, to mount is to place or fix (an object) in its operating position. While a mounting is a backing, setting, or support for something.

> *Meanwhile, God's firm foundation is as firm as ever, these sentences engraved on the stones: god knows who belongs to him. spurn evil, all you who name god as god. In a well-furnished kitchen there are not only crystal goblets and silver platters, but waste cans and compost buckets- some out the garbage. Become the kind of container God can use to present any and every kind of gift to his guests for their blessing. Run away from infantile indulgence. Run after mature righteousness- faith, love, peace- joining those who are in honest and serious prayer before God. Refuse to get involved in inane discussions; they always end up in fights. God's servant must not be argumentative, but a gentle listener and a teacher who keeps cool, working firmly but patiently with those who refuse to obey. You never know how or when God might sober them up with a change of heart and a turning to the truth, enabling them to escape the Devil's trap, where they are caught and held captive, forced to run his errands.*
> *2 Timothy 2:19-26 MSG*

When something is mounted, it becomes stable. While I was in therapy, I remember having a difficult time describing my experiences of processing everything. It was more than an emotion. I was confused. The best way I could describe it was to envision and a 15-story building... a mansion. Each year of our relationship from beginning was represented by a floor of a building. The building itself was adorned with beautiful landscaping and window adornments, allowing people to admire it and sometimes look inside. We let just enough light inside. It had a pretty door. The brick and mortar were our love and commonalities, everything that we experienced separate of each other in childhood, together in relationship, and the future we planned when vision building. Eventually, the building becomes very tall with each passing year.

There are also cracks, not visible to the naked eye. Cracks in the foundation that grew, hidden from the naked eye.

I was comfortable. I was on the 15th floor and my husband was creeping, out of the side door. When his secret was revealed, it was if a bulldozer drove right through that mansion, bringing it crashing down to rubble and smoke. Ultimately resulting in a catastrophic mess. Memories torn and damaged, some buried underneath the mess. And I got many bruises from falling from such a high level. This was literally was rock bottom.

Having to express that and say exactly how I perceived it to be was freeing for me.

The way I made sense of it being possible to heal and recover was to imagine I was sorting through the rubble and picking out what could be salvaged, which was exhausting. I couldn't do it by myself. My support allowed me to decide, with clarity, what I wanted, without grabbing onto just anything to feel normal again. We rebuilt with a restored foundation, Christ. And also, with a 'screw' that, like a trophy, went straight through the center of our marriage. That screw is our will, lined up with God's will. Rahsaan and I made sure to learn how to love each other and ourselves the way God intended.

It starts with intentionality. Google dictionary says intentionality is *the fact of being deliberate or purposive.*

We deliberately loved on each other. We sent each other pictures and little notes. We did surprise deliveries and acts of service. Foundational stuff that easily gets tossed to the left when you have responsibilities of work and family. I took it a step further to be deliberate with what I said to myself and allowed others to say to me. I was deliberate about how I dressed and how I thought and all the things that I love to do for me. Again, very basic stuff. Stuff that we did before.

We were intentional of a Christ-centered marriage and life. Rahsaan had to get back to his relationship with Christ; seek and learn how God wanted a wife to be cared for and honored. Also, in turn, I had to be deliberate in being the wife he needed and deserved. A friend of mine put it perfectly. She said: *"As a woman of Christ, I establish that Christ is King through His word. The Bible gives us the blueprint of how we should live our lives."* Ephesians 5:22-23 states, *"Wives, submit to your own husbands, as to the Lord. For the husband is head of the wife, as also Christ is head of the church; and He is the Savior of the body."* If we truly meditated on this scripture, we would ask ourselves, *"Would I question Christ? Would I complain and condemn him? Would I be too busy to answer Christ's call or respond? Wouldn't I trust him? Wouldn't I praise him all the time, and show gratitude and thanks?"* These questions would make us realize that we are hurting our marriage by not fully surrendering to *GOD*! It has nothing to do with your husband. If you surrender to *GOD*, then you have *NO* expectations of *MAN*.

In the mounting process, I relied on the Lord to guide me and show me His will for my life and our marriage.

I am who I am, doing what God called me to do, including who God called me to be in my marriage. Being not only a help for my husband, but also a servant to women globally for Christ through my work. Walking out *MY* purpose and complementing his. They don't have to be separate, as I fought so long to do.

What does a Christ-centered life look like? It looks like praying, without ceasing. It looks like being bold. It looks like being on the same page as God and being available to Him for his use. It looks like setting boundaries and commandments for yourself and relying on the Holy Spirit to guide and teach you self-control and discipline.

It looks like being broken for a good greater than yourself. And allowing your flesh to die so that you won't be led astray by it.

And what does a Christ-centered marriage look like? All of the previously mentioned, placing your spouse in the middle instead of just you. It looks like a partnership with Christ as the coach, comforter, healer, lawyer, etc.

When we were rummaging through the mess, deciding what could stay and what had to be thrown out, we decided to also hit the reset button on the years of marriage we had prior to the destruction. We started planning a vow renewal. We thought *"here's our chance to really go into this assignment with clarity on exactly what we want and how we want it."* Out with the old, in with the new. This time knowing for certain that we BOTH want to be in our marriage. We made our plans, picked out a venue, color scheme, menu, guest list, and all.

At the same time, God gave me work to do. I started writing and working on the I'm Every Woman event. I woke up one morning, and God said to bring the women together, to stop thinking about it and just do it. When you're mounted, the excuses are null and void. So, I was obedient and just did it. I went for it and participated in the birthing of a ministry.

God showed me how our betrayers are often our midwives. Because of their betrayal, they participate in the birthing of a blessing. God attracted so many through my healing process and every time I ministered to a woman I thought of how many go through things while another in close proximity of her has the keys to her freedom, yet she will never know it because she is still in bondage to it. The *I'm Every Woman* event served as a safe space for women to connect, heal, and grow.

I ended up scrapping my plans for our vow renewal. I absolutely had no time to plan. But God did. He placed a vision in Rahsaan's heart. Rahsaan ended up surprising me with a secret renewal ceremony. He told me that we were invited to dinner with the pastor who handled our counseling, along with his wife. He was adamant about going to dinner. The only problem with this was dinner was two and a half hours of travel one way, and it was pouring down rain. We were in the middle of a storm. I didn't want to do anything or go anywhere. My nails weren't done. I couldn't figure out my hair. And I had nothing to wear. In spite of all of that, he insisted on us going and got me out of the house.

As we pulled up to the church, I started seeing familiar cars, but honestly thought maybe it was just a coincidence. We walked in and we were greeted with 50 of our family members and friends, all dressed in black and white. Black representing the death of our old selves and white representing the birth of the new us! The biggest surprise for me was seeing a face I hadn't seen for a very long time: my father. He came to the front of the crowd and we hugged and cried. It was a moment I yearned for and didn't even realize until it happened. See, when we were

first married my father was incarcerated. It was one of
the hardest decisions I had to make: to wait until he was
released for him to be there and give me away or move
forward and deal with his absence. I chose the latter out
of fear. And a small part of me carried that for years. I
still felt like I was robbed of an opportunity for my dad
to show up for me. Rahsaan said God pressed his heart to
reach out to my dad and give us the opportunity of taking
that walk again. I will forever remember that moment. It
led me to write a letter to him. That moment gave me the
closure that I never knew I needed.

A letter to my earthly father

*Today is your 56th Birthday. What a blessing
from God to see this new year of your life. In
a time when so many of your generation have
not made it. I don't have many memories of us.
There's truth in the statement "a daughter's
love for her father never changes." Immature
decisions, drugs, and jail kept us apart. Even
though you disappointed me over and over,
my love for you has never changed. I think it
helped that my mother never spoke badly about
you in my presence, especially when she wiped
my tears after the disappointment hit me again.
Sometimes I envied my friends growing up who
had/have their fathers. And I noticed the same
spirit with my adult friends' relationships
with their fathers. And somewhere in my 20s,
I forgave you. I always pray for you. Having
a relationship with my heavenly Father taught*

me about forgiveness. I learned to release the burden of pain of growing up without you because God taught me that it hurt me more than you by holding onto it.

Then I met the love of my life and he shared a similar upbringing. You weren't there when I took his last name on June 4, 2005. Most of your bad choices and habits caught up with you and took you away for some years. And I prayed about that missed opportunity for you. And on June 4, 2015, Rahsaan surprised me with a vow renewal. But the biggest surprise was seeing you there, waiting for your chance to give me away to my groom. And even though I still don't see you, that memory is forever etched in my heart. I don't hate you. Grace and Mercy taught me that life happens to us all and at any given moment a bad decision can be made to send you on the wrong path. I am blessed to have a heavenly Father who stood in your void. His love for me has guided me and protected me my entire life. I pray you are well. And I forever love you

Father of the fatherless and protector of widows is God in his holy habitation. Psalm 68:5 ESV

For my father and my mother have forsaken me, but the Lord will take me in. Psalm 27:10 ESV

Our renewal represented and gave us a refreshing change.

It also confirmed what God had appointed. A Christ-centered marriage also requires intentionality of what it is at its core and not just a good look for the 'gram (Instagram). 'relationship goals' have become a part of the culture craze with social media. Since social media was the initial gateway into our marriage for the other woman, we also had to be very intentional about what we gave the world a look into. I had to be very intentional about what I shared online. Only showing and posting what God led me to reveal. To be clear, I wasn't living or operating in fear. I let wisdom lead. Everything is not for everybody. Some people sit around looking for something to tear apart and sow discord into. We realized that she used a lot of what I posted as weight to get in the door. Not excusing him one bit, however people covet what they see online. It is vital that you stay connected to your foundation, your mounting and with the screw, your will to God's will, intact! You must stay connected. Otherwise you will fall over and break!

Marriage brings out the best and the worst in us and it certainly can't cure us. It requires us to humble ourselves often, listen more, serve more, love more, pray more, give more & give our spouse to Jesus. We must let go of the fantasy that marriage is perfect. And that marriage makes us perfect. Sometimes, you have to make up in your mind that your marriage is perfect for you. Stop comparing & work out your own salvation in your marriage. Work on you. Then God works on your spouse. God can resurrect a dead marriage! Start to see resurrection differently. See its design to reset your marriage and move you forward. There are some things that God wants to do with you, that have died and will begin to move again from God's resurrecting power.

I hear *'relationship goals'* a lot when it comes to us. To continue in transparency, it makes me a little uncomfortable because I know it isn't easy and I pray that people see God and not us. God is real and His love is everlasting. He loves us. Not because of anything we've done or have not done. He loves us because He *IS* God. Period. His love overcomes everything. When you put Him first and build a three-stranded cord, you become a knot, that's not easily broken. Dying of self and striving to become more like Christ daily, that's relationship goals! I've also heard that you shouldn't be with someone who tries to change you. And vice versa. However, you can simply inspire your mate to be better, thus promoting and encouraging change and growth. The major key is to do it together so that you don't grow apart. Rahsaan has changed me. I have changed him. Better yet we've inspired each other to change! I'm glad we aren't the same people we were 20 years ago. 10 years ago. Last year. Even the day before yesterday! We're getting better, together, giving each other our best selves and representing God's power. And most importantly, staying connected to the mounting!!!

My perspective of our mansion crumbling to the ground allowed us to rebuild, this time with God instructing us and guiding us brick by brick. We fell in love with each other again, but we also fell in love with God. We fell in love with the way we were both nurtured, showing us what true unconditional love looks and behaves and feels like. We both arrived at a place where absolutely nothing could compromise our loyalty and faithfulness to God. I even told Rahsaan that although he's 'first', he's second. Second to my relationship with Christ. And he eventually ended up being the same way with me. Putting Christ at the center allows us to serve each other better. If I wouldn't ignore Christ, I can't ignore my husband. If I talk to Christ throughout the day, guess what? I talk to my husband throughout the day.

Being mounted also means being still. It means being quiet. God fights our battles, so there's no need to talk or explain or justify anything! Maintain your posture in this part, as you won't have to bend over or climb down to address anything. Others may question: how is that you've gone through all that you've gone through and is still standing? God will show them, so you won't have to. He will fight your battles. You have to stay in position and heed to his direction. You are now building! Building for God's kingdom. You no longer have the time or power to waste to stop and address everything that comes your way. Stay in position!

When you are mounted, you are now in your operating position! This means to be clear and accepting of the purpose and call God has commanded you to do. There is no more time for second-guessing or doubting yourself. To be in this position means that you have completely given yourself over to God's will over your life. This includes your trials and triumphs. Who needs what you have? Who is going through a storm and is praying for what you have inside of you? To be mounted means you have labored, pushed, and have begun to birth what The Lord has shown you! Your gifts are fortified when released. The more you serve, the stronger they become.

Being mounted also means studying and applying the Word of God. A Christ-centered life/marriage comes with Godly counsel and wisdom. Everyone has advice, but not everyone has Godly counsel. You have to ask and discern. Godly wisdom comes with a proven track record. Be mounted and be mindful of who speaks over your new life. These people will ask you *"have you prayed about it?"* before even offering advice. With them, their Godly wisdom looks beyond the mess and looks inside, offering not just an opinion, but The Word of God!

We were intentional about who invited into our lives. We sought out solid, married couples to pray for and with and keep each other accountable. And let me tell you how this played out in my life! I boldly went before God and made my request for ordained friendships clear. My prayer went like this:

> *Father, I love you and I thank you. I thank you for using me and keeping me for your purpose. Lord, let my strength be in you to recognize who YOU sent to me and to rebuke who you did not send. I only want those ordained, anointed AND appointed connections. Send me whoever is for me. Thank you, Father.*
>
> *Amen.*

And they all showed up! I have a core group of women that is assigned to me and I to them. We cover each other, we hold each other accountable and we war for each other. We don't talk often, but when we do the power overflows, and vision elevates! They see and they speak the truth to me, for me and over me. Once mounted, I no longer had time for looking over my shoulder, keeping up with who's against me and who's jealous or vengeful. I just can't do that anymore. I'd rather that energy goes towards what is helping me grow. When mounted, you are certain of your power and identity. You know the truth and you lead in love. It all aligns with the pure, unadulterated, Holy Word of God. And you don't want part of anything that excludes Him. We have to be certain when we say we belong to him, and know that everything we do matters. How we represent Him is supreme over all of the other stuff. Period.

In slightly over 13 years of marriage, we've had days where it was Heaven on Earth. And we've had days that were hell. There were obviously days we wanted to quit. However, those days we wanted to quit pressed us and developed us and made us better. They brought us both closer to Jesus. Traditional vows say for better or worse. What happens when better or worse is tested? You push through and take the only person you can control (yourself) to Jesus and let Him work on you. What God put together NO person, NO money, NO hardship, NO friends, NO job, NO kids, NO depression, NO fear, NO demon can tear apart. IF He put it together, then He will keep it together! No weapon formed against you will prosper. Pray for your spouse and your marriage. Love hard. Fight hard. Pray hard. It's your superpower.

Accepting Christ as my Lord and Savior gives me eternal life in Heaven, as well as foundation while living and navigating on earth, and at the same time allows me to experience freedom from the shame, insecurities, guilt and much more associated with my past. All of this is by grace, which comes from Christ when I submit to Him.

What almost broke me actually released the little girl that was hiding behind the labels that so many put on top of me over the years; the little girl that had dreams and visions of greatness and purpose. The girl who knew who she was before the world told her who she should be. I choose to be transparent so that you don't see me, but you see Christ in me. I am far from perfect, but I love me because He first loves me. I am worthy of it and so are you! When you know who you are and whose you are, you WIN. Our self-worth is not for sale, the price was paid at the cross. Be free! Validation is for parking! You have already been certified and stamped! Now move your feet in boldness!

You are ready. You are ready to light the world with your fire! You are not confined to who you were, who you are now, or who others expect you to be. At any given time, you can reinvent yourself and become a new and improved you. You are never stuck in one place. You can evolve, change, and grow at any time that you want to. You are not confined to labels or other people's expectations. Each day is a new opportunity to learn more and once you know better, you owe it to yourself to do better. Be free to grow into the best you!

You have been molded and are now aware of your identity. You have been refined, fire tried and certified, having gone through the fire while all things that were not of God purged out of you. You have been polished, shining, therefore every word out of your mouth and action performed now reflects Him. And you have been mounted, rooted in the foundation of the word of God and aligned with pure truth.

You are a trophy made of gold. A reward. A prize and asset to the kingdom as well as this earth. You are not to be handled just any way.

Conclusion

WHEN I RECEIVED THE VISION to write this book, I had no idea the journey and process it would take me on to get it completed. I started out with hopes of just telling part of my story as a reference point of healing for other women who have gone through the same thing. I became passionate about helping others save their marriage.

I have poured out my spirit in this body of work, praying that it touches and wins at least one soul. Praying that it changes at least one marriage. Praying that it restores at least one woman's view of herself. And empowers her to walk in the fullness of her identity in Christ.

This is year four of my journey of writing this book, my journey of shedding the layers of who I thought I was and facing the mirror of my authentic self. It is my journey of hearing and accepting who God called me to be, waking up in the middle of the night with revelation and scripture of who I am. And by His grace, the light He has placed in me, that anointing now shines as inspiration for others.

It is hard to describe the joy and discomfort that I feel simultaneously, simply because most will only see it on the surface. These are growing pains. The more I seek Him, the more I "un-become" who I was and become who He designed me to be.

I was completely uncomfortable writing this book, but I have never wanted anything more than to be a beacon of light and vessel of God. An example to show what being tried in the fire and coming out unscathed looks like! Be encouraged, my sister. Have faith that if He did it for me, He will do it for you!

Acknowledgements

To my husband: I loved you then, I love you now, and I will love you forever. Thank you for loving me back to life. Thank you for seeking God to understand the gift of a wife and committing to never forgetting it; for understanding who you are and are called to do. Your growth and walk with God have been glorious to witness. Thank you for confronting your demons and healing, and most of all for giving me your blessing to release this book! Everything comes together when we give the pieces over to God. I see you. I see your determination to be a great man. And I thank you. Your encouragement is what pushed me and got me through the completion of this book.

Love is an act of endless forgiveness. Forgiveness is me giving up my right to hurt you for hurting me. Forgiveness is the final act of love.

I dedicate this body of work to our children.

To our daughters, I pray that you never experience the pain I felt in becoming. However, should this 'story' cross your doorstep and enter your home, I pray you each seek The Lord and find wisdom and courage to fight and press toward your good; just as God promises.

To our one and only son: I pray you have a wonderful example of marriage in your dad and me. That you look to your earthly AND heavenly father for guidance on how to be a man. A man that will honor his wife and cherish her.

Children, as your mother, I pray that I continue to teach you all who you are and help you understand what you're made of, especially when life hits you. My parenting goal is to give you a childhood that you won't have to heal from as an adult. Parenting is challenging, and I love you all so much. I am honored to be your mother and continue to fight for you.

To my mother Jackie: thank you for not letting me repeat your mistakes. You have forever been honest with me and transparent about your own personal struggles and victories. You are the reason why I look for the good in people. Your transparency provided a map for me, that's helped me throughout my adult life. You provided me the keys and compass to unlock what was hidden and break generational curses in our family. You didn't go through what you went through for me to just be average. You deserve to see me birth greatness and restore royal identity. Your courage makes me proud to be your daughter. I love you.

For my sisters, my tribe, my anointed and appointed gems; who gave me your shoulder when I needed to cry, your ear when I needed to scream or make sense of my new normal, or even your *"I'll bail you out or be sitting right next to you"* when thoughts of revenge came to mind: thank you for being my keeper. Thank you for straightening my crown when it shifted, and helping me hold my head up when it became too heavy to wear. Thank you for pushing me and not letting me settle in my mess. Thank you for all of your constant prayers, encouragement, and sometimes tough love to push through this and get this book completed. My tribe is amazing!

To Dr. Karen Bethea: you are a true gem. You entered my life when I was healing and finding myself, after accepting the calling on my life. I struggled greatly with being that powerful woman and still honoring my husband without making him inferior. You have taught me to be a wife and not a knife; to be his wife and not his priest. The way you love, serve and honor Pastor Linwood is incomparable and a godly example for us all. Thank you.

And to the *'other woman'*: I sincerely thank you. The greatest pain I have ever experienced ultimately birthed my purpose and brought it full throttle. As I healed, I saw your pain, resentment, and envy. *'Hurt people hurt people.'* It softened my heart towards you. It raised that fire in which I had intentionally buried deep down inside of me some time long ago. It brought my boldness back; the boldness to love and let the light of God in me shine brighter than ever. The boldness to believe again. I pray you are freed from your demons, healed, and that you truly know that God loves you. Your worth is far worth more than rubies...

ERICA GRIER is an entrepreneur, author, visionary and midwife of purpose to women. It was through her career in cosmetology that she discovered her calling and connection to women of all backgrounds and ages, inspiring them to walk in authenticity while restoring and maintaining the beauty in their crowns. She is the founder of the women's empowerment movement, I'm Every Woman, where she inspires women to be bold, fearless, powerful, confident, and determined through brunch events and letters of power through email.

Erica is happily married to her high school sweetheart Rahsaan. Together they have four beautiful children and currently reside in Atlanta.

Follow Erica on
Facebook @ Erica Grier
Instagram @ericagrier and @theericagrierexperience
Twitter @ericagrier

Made in the USA
Middletown, DE
02 September 2023

37553085R00068